Seven

CONTINENTS

of the World

ASIA

By Tracy Vonder Brink

A Crabtree Crown Book

Crabtree Publishing

crabtreebooks.com

School-to-Home Support for Caregivers and Teachers

This appealing book is designed to teach students about core subject areas. Students will build upon what they already know about the subject, and engage in topics that they want to learn more about. Here are a few guiding questions to help readers build their comprehensions skills. Possible answers appear here in red.

Before Reading:

What do I know about Asia?

- *I know Asia is a continent.*
- *I know China is part of Asia.*

What do I want to learn about this topic?

- *I want to know how many languages are spoken in Asia.*
- *I want to learn about animals that live in Asia.*

During Reading:

I'm curious to know...

- *I'm curious to know what kind of foods Asians eat.*
- *I'm curious to know what sports Asians enjoy.*

How is this like something I already know?

- *I know what foods people who live near me eat.*
- *I know what sports I like to play.*

After Reading:

What was the author trying to teach me?

- *The author was trying to teach me about Asia's landforms.*
- *The author was trying to teach me about Asian countries.*

How did the photographs and captions help me understand more?

- *The photographs helped me picture Asia.*
- *The captions gave me extra information.*

TABLE OF CONTENTS

CHAPTER 1
GET TO KNOW ASIA

What continent has two of the highest points on Earth? Where do monkeys climb and lotus flowers bloom? Where do more than 4 billion people live?

Asia!

Mount Fuji is Japan's highest mountain.

Almost all of Asia lies north of the **equator**. Asia contains about one-third of all land on Earth. It also has the longest coast of any continent.

The world has seven continents. Asia is the largest.

OCEANS AND ISLANDS

The Arctic Ocean splashes against Asia's north. The Indian Ocean lies to its south. The Pacific Ocean washes up on Asia's east. Europe **borders** its west. The Red Sea divides Asia from Africa, and the Bering Strait separates Asia from North America.

Asia has thousands of islands. The countries of Japan and the Philippines are made up of many islands. Sri Lanka, Singapore, and Indonesia are also Asian island nations.

Japan is a string of about 7,000 islands. Only around 400 have people. Most of Japan's people live on its 5 main islands.

CHAPTER 2
LANDFORMS AND CLIMATE

Asia's size means it has many types of land. It has mountain ranges. It also has deserts. Asia has **plateaus** and large areas of flatlands. It also has rivers and lakes.

The Tibetan Plateau is called "The Roof of the World." It covers an area almost half the size of the United States.

MOUNTAINS

The Himalaya mountain range stretches through the countries of India, Nepal, and Bhutan. Mount Everest, the tallest mountain peak on Earth, is part of the Himalayas. K2 is the second-highest mountain in the world. It is also in Asia.

DESERTS AND PLAINS

The Gobi is Asia's largest desert. It covers parts of Mongolia and China. The Gobi is mostly bare rock. The Rub'al-Khali is the world's largest sand desert. It stretches across four Asian countries. The West Siberian Plain is one of the world's largest flatland areas. It is in Russia.

The Gobi Desert holds many dinosaur fossils.

The Yangtze is China's most important river. Nearly half of China's crops are grown in the plains around the river.

WATERS

The Yangtze is Asia's longest river. It runs through China. The Tigris and Euphrates rivers begin in Turkey, flow through Syria and Iraq, and empty into the Persian Gulf. Lake Baikal is in Russia. Lake Baikal is the world's deepest lake.

CLIMATE

Almost every **climate** in the world can be found in Asia. The far north is cold **tundra**. The continent's south is warm and **tropical**. Grasslands lie between the tundra and the tropics. Some areas are deserts.

Siberia, Russia, is known for its cold temperatures and long winters.

Monsoons are seasonal winds that last for several months. The winds are full of moisture and bring heavy rains to parts of Asia.

Summer winds bring rain to the south and to some Asian islands. Between 80 to 85% of the year's rain in those areas falls during this time. **Typhoons** sometimes develop over the warm waters of the Northwest Pacific Ocean. These storms bring dangerous winds and heavy rain.

CHAPTER 3
NATURAL RESOURCES

Nearly every important **mineral** can be found in Asia. China, Siberia, and India contain more than half the world's coal. Oil is found in the Middle East. Coal and oil are important fuel and energy sources. The continent also has iron, gold, and other metals. Forests supply valuable wood.

Rice is grown in a flooded field called a paddy.

Asia grows almost all of the world's rice. It also produces the most tea in the world. Wheat is grown in northern China. Most fruits and vegetables grown on the continent are eaten locally, but some bananas, pineapples, and coconuts are sold to other countries.

CHAPTER 4
PLANTS AND ANIMALS

Bamboo has been grown and used in Asia for thousands of years. Bamboo is used for food, clothes, furniture, and even musical instruments.

PLANTS

Asia is home to many different types of plants. China alone has around 30,000 different **species**. Parts of Asia have the largest bamboo forests in the world. Japan is known for its cherry blossom trees.

The lotus flower is important to some Asian religions. It is a symbol of hope because the plant grows in muddy waters yet makes a beautiful flower. The flowers may be white, pink, yellow, red, blue, or purple. Lotus flowers may bloom all year in Southeast Asia.

ANIMALS OF THE RAIN FOREST

The rain forests of Southeast Asia are home to many monkeys. Macaques and langurs hide in the trees. The long-nosed proboscis monkey is a surprisingly strong swimmer. Orangutans, a kind of great ape, are only found in these rain forests.

Crested black macaques are only found on two islands in Indonesia.

Some Asian animals are in danger of dying out. Human activities such as cutting down trees and clearing land for crops destroys where these animals live. Orangutans and tigers are among those in danger.

ANIMALS OF THE MOUNTAINS

Arctic foxes, wolves, and caribou have thick fur to keep warm in the cold north. Ibex goats' sharp, curved hooves help them climb steep rock. Yaks can breathe even in high mountains where the air is thin.

Arctic foxes hunt lemmings. Lemmings are in the mouse family. Arctic foxes leap up and dive headfirst into the snow to catch them.

Giant pandas live in the mountains of southwestern China. Their thick fur helps keep them warm. Giant pandas spend at least 12 hours every day eating bamboo. Their back teeth are broad and flat to crush it. Giant pandas eat both the leaves and the stems.

CHAPTER 5

COUNTRIES AND CITIES

Some countries also have land in more than one continent. Most of Russia is in Asia, but some of its land is in Europe. Russia is still considered part of Asia.

The Maldives is an island nation in the Indian Ocean.

COUNTRIES

Asia has between 45 and 53 countries. The number isn't exact because while some areas consider themselves countries, others disagree. For example, Taiwan considers itself independent, but China counts Taiwan as part of China.

China and Russia have the most land in Asia. China and India have the most people. More than two billion people live in China and India combined. Maldives, an island country in the Indian Ocean, is the smallest Asian country. Fewer than 600,000 people live there.

CITIES

Nearly half of Asia's people still live in the countryside. But its cities grow larger every day. Tokyo, Japan, is the world's largest city. Around 37 million people live there. Delhi, India, has a population of around 30 million. Shanghai, China, holds about 27 million people.

A megacity is a city where more than 10 million people live. Asia has 23 megacities.

Big cities offer better jobs, more schools, and more opportunities than small towns and villages. But cities are also often overcrowded. Some who live there are very poor. Cars, factories, and power plants may dirty the air.

CHAPTER 6
CULTURE AND PEOPLE

Asia's cultures are different from region to region. South Asia is home to many cultures and language groups, including Hindi and Tamil. People of Arab, Iranian, and other backgrounds live in the Middle East. China, Korea, and Japan share East Asian culture. More than 2,000 different languages are spoken in Asia.

The camel is Saudi Arabia's national animal.

Religions have special days. Hindus mark the end of winter with the Holi festival. They throw colored powder to celebrate spring.

The world's major religions started in Asia. Christianity and Judaism began in the Middle East. Islam also started there. Hinduism and Buddhism both began in India. All continue to be practiced in Asia today.

FOOD

Many Asian countries have favorite foods. Russians enjoy thin, delicate pancakes called blini. Indians cook biryani, a spiced mix of meat and rice. The Japanese roll seafood in rice to make sushi. Dondurma is a thick Turkish ice cream.

It takes 10 years of training to become a master sushi chef in Japan.

SPORTS

Sports are played all over the continent. Basketball and table tennis are popular in China. The people of India and Pakistan love cricket. Soccer is popular nearly everywhere.

GLOSSARY

border (BOR-dr): The place where one area ends and another starts

climate (KLAI-muht): The usual weather conditions in a certain region or area

equator (EE-kway-tr): An imaginary line around the middle of Earth that is the same distance from the North Pole to the South Pole

mineral (MIH-nuh-rl): A solid substance that is formed naturally under the ground

plateau (pla-TOW): A broad area of high, flat land

species (SPEE-sheez or SPEE-sees): A group of animals or plants that are alike in certain ways

tropical (TRAH-puh-kl): Of or having to do with the part of the world near the equator where the weather is very warm

tundra (TUHN-druh): A large, flat plain without trees in cold northern parts of the world

typhoon (tai-FOON): A large, powerful, destructive storm that begins in the western Pacific

INDEX

COMPREHENSION QUESTIONS

1. How many people live in Asia?
   a. More than 4 billion
   b. About 100 million
   c. Fewer than 2 million
2. Which Asian animal eats mostly bamboo?
   a. Orangutan
   b. Ibex goat
   c. Giant panda
3. What city has the most people in Asia?
   a. Delhi, India
   b. Tokyo, Japan
   c. Shanghai, China
4. True or False: Almost all of Asia lies north of the equator.
5. True of False: The Yangtze is Asia's longest river.

Answers: 1. A, 2. C, 3. B, 4. True, 5. True

ABOUT THE AUTHOR

Tracy Vonder Brink loves true stories and facts. She has written more than 20 books for kids and is a contributing editor for three children's science magazines. Tracy lives in Cincinnati, Ohio, with her husband, two daughters, and two rescue dogs.

Crabtree Publishing

crabtreebooks.com 800-387-7650

 In Canada: We acknowledge the financial support of the Government of Canada through the Canada Book Fund for our publishing activities.

Written by: Tracy Vonder Brink
Cover design by: Kathy Walsh
Interior design by: Kathy Walsh
Series Development: James Earley
Proofreader: Crystal Sikkens
Educational Consultant: Marie Lemke M.Ed.
Print coordinator: Katherine Kantor

Hardcover	978-1-0396-6052-6
Paperback	978-1-0396-6247-6
Ebook (pdf)	978-1-0396-7043-3
Epub	978-1-0396-7241-3
Read-along	978-1-0396-7439-4

Printed in Canada/022024/CP20240215

Library and Archives Canada Cataloguing in Publication
Title: Asia / by Tracy Vonder Brink.
Names: Vonder Brink, Tracy, author.
Description: Series statement: Seven continents of the world | "A Crabtree crown book". | Includes index.
Identifiers: Canadiana (print) 202204122354 | Canadiana (ebook) 20220422362 | ISBN 9781039660526 (hardcover) | ISBN 9781039662476 (softcover) | ISBN 9781039670433 (PDF) | ISBN 9781039672413 (EPUB) | ISBN 9781039674394 (read-along ebook)
Subjects: LCSH: Asia—Geography—Juvenile literature. | LCSH: Asia—Juvenile literature.
Classification: LCC DS5.92 .V66 2023 | DDC j915—dc23

Published in Canada
Crabtree Publishing
616 Welland Avenue
St. Catharines, Ontario
L2M 5V6

Published in the United States
Crabtree Publishing
347 Fifth Avenue
Suite 1402-145
New York, NY 10016

Photographs: Shutterstock; Cover: ©Triff, ©Khurasan, ©nypl, @Dima_designer, ©Daniel Prudek; Title Pg: ©Triff, ©Dima_designer; Pg 3-31: ©Triff; Pg 4-31: ©WinWin artlab; Pg 4: ©Travel mania; Pg 6: ©siro46; Pg 8: © Iryna Hromotska; Pg 9: ©HelloRF Zcool; Pg 10: ©aleksander hunta; Pg 11: ©Pawika Tongtavee; Pg 12: ©Andrei Stepanov; Pg 13: ©Daniel J. Rao; Pg 14: ©StevenK; Pg 15: ©Tompix; Pg 16: ©Patryk Kosmider; Pg 17:©anek.soowannaphoom, ©visualLEH; Pg 18: ©Sergey Uryadnikov; Pg 19: ©Yusnizam Yusof, ©Ondrej Prosicky, ©lukaszemanphoto; Pg 20: ©Andrew Astbury, ©Angelica Klingberg; Pg 21 © PHOTO BY LOLA; Pg 22: ©Andrei Minsk; Pg 23: ©Skycolors; Pg 24: ©karinkamon; Pg 25: ©Patryk Kosmider; Pg 26: ©AFZAL KHAN MAHEEN; Pg 27: ©nelle hembry; Pg 28: ©Catherine77; Pg 29: ©Stefan Holm

Library of Congress Cataloging-in-Publication Data
Names: Vonder Brink, Tracy, author.
Title: Asia / Tracy Vonder Brink.
Description: New York, NY : Crabtree Publishing, [2023] | Series: Seven continents of the world | "A Crabtree crown book."
Identifiers: LCCN 2022041840 (print) | LCCN 2022041841 (ebook) | ISBN 9781039660526 (hardcover) | ISBN 9781039662476 (paperback) | ISBN 9781039670433 (ebook) | ISBN 9781039672413 (epub) | ISBN 9781039674394
Subjects: LCSH: Asia--Juvenile literature.
Classification: LCC DS5 .V66 2023 (print) | LCC DS5 (ebook) | DDC 950--dc23/eng/20220831
LC record available at https://lccn.loc.gov/2022041840
LC ebook record available at https://lccn.loc.gov/2022041841